Inspiration
for the
Heart
of a
Woman

*A Refreshing Approach
to Embracing Your Greatness*

Crystal Lawrence

Inspiration for the Heart of a Woman
A Refreshing Approach to
Embracing Your Greatness

ISBN-13: 978-1721219339

ISBN-10: 1721219331

A woman's presence is her greatness.

Remarkably and wondrously made is she.
(Psalm 139:13-14)

Dedications

To God
The *center* of my joy and my *greatest* inspiration

In loving memory of my mother, Barbara Ann Fields
The extraordinary woman who will always be
the inspiration of my heart
She showed me the true meaning of love
and how to *embrace my greatness*

In loving memory of my father, Thomas Edward Shaw
Forever my Hero

To my deeply loved
Husband, Son, and Grandson
You are *every beat* of my heart
I love you beyond words

To my beautiful Sister
There is *no* bond or love like ours

To my precious immediate and extended family
Thank you for blessing my life with a *rich legacy* of togetherness
The strength of our love is engrained in my soul

To my dearest friends
Your kindness, prayers, listening ears, and invaluable
encouragement made my book a beautiful reality
I simply *adore* you

To *you* of course — *extraordinary woman*
Apart from the essence of your presence
such a labor of love could not have emerged

Unforgettable Expressions

"What a joyous feast for women is this book! Reading it is like sitting down at a comfortably elegant table of delights while you are served up delectable small plates of love, faith, inspiration, wisdom, humor, and immeasurable devotion to cultivating your own inherent greatness. Every page is filled with replenishing morsels to savor time and again. Grab your box of tissues: Crystal Lawrence's love arrow is headed straight toward every woman's heart!"
—Rachel Snyder, Author
365 Words of Well-Being for Women

"This is beautiful work. It takes me directly to a need, which is self-care and encouragement as a woman of faith. It tells 'how to' with gentle instruction. I like your word rhythm. It speaks confidence that you know of what you speak."
—Yvonnie Dockery
St. Stephen Missionary Baptist Church

"I'm not biased when I say you have penned a ministering masterpiece. I got lost in my favorites. Each one seemed to get better and better. What I appreciate the most is your range through the variety. You go wide and shallow with some (*Timeout*) and then deep and narrow with others (*Take a Breather*). Your spin on the (*Liquid Sunshine*) just grabs you!"
—Anthony L. Dockery, Pastor
St. Stephen Missionary Baptist Church

"Inspiration for the Heart of a Woman" exudes love, wisdom, and nourishment. All women will be inspired by this read. But for motherless women, like me, this book mends the heart, giving us empowering tools to BECOME who we wish we had. "Inspiration for the Heart of a Woman" reigned true to its title. For that, I am thankful, refueled, and equipped to continue to serve and uplift those in need."
—Trinity Wallace-Ellis
Resilient One & Associates
CEO, Professional Trainer & Inspirational Speaker

"This book is so you! It's beautiful, authentic and straight from your heart. You are truly inspired by the Spirit and live your life by your words. I also know it's not been without struggle and learning by experience. You are, and will continue to be an inspiration to women (and men) and your family through these words."
—Alice Beirne
Professional Consultant

"In reading this love letter to ALL women, I recognize Crystal's heart. She is full of compassion, strength, wisdom, and honors Sisterhood. At the initial opening, I felt as if I should turn on my smooth jazz, grab a hot cup of tea, and celebrate Womanhood. "Inspiration for the Heart of a Woman: A Refreshing Approach to Embracing Your Greatness" is exactly what is needed at this time in our culture. This is an authentic, gracious, and moving piece of work. God's hand is on this woman."
—Laura A. Franklin, Author
The Preacher and the Princess

Contents

Contents

Relax, Release, Relate

Share The Wealth

Contents

For The Greater Good

Make The Most Of Your Journey

Contents

Live In The Moment

Be An Enduring Light

Introduction

You are extraordinary — unequivocally so!

Embracing your greatness simply means valuing your presence: the glorious blessing of being a woman.

As you embark on what is sure to be an inspiring journey, reserve for yourself a space of solitude to take a few gentle deep breaths, quiet your mind, surrender your cares, and simply relax and *be* in this moment, this space, this time.

From my heart to yours,
Crystal

Comfy ~ Cozy

So delighted
we have this time together

Feel free to share everything
there is to know about you —
your life, your hopes, your dreams
and I'll do the same

We'll bare our souls into the wee hours
talking about whatever comes to mind
especially if it comforts our hearts
and puts smiles on our faces

No subject is off limits
every concern will be embraced —
your cares are my cares
your joys are my joys

Now relax yourself
have a cuppa tea and a warm croissant
and let's enjoy the blessing
of each other's company

Your Greatness Precedes You

You are God's perfect and most loved masterpiece —
the very apple of His eye. That alone affirms your greatness!

Make no mistake about it, your greatness truly does precede you. By *Divine design* you were created to grace this world with every wondrous fiber of your being. There remains no question of your inherent greatness. You are a *heavenly fusion* of heart, mind, body, and soul!

Quintessential Woman

You inspire the world many times over

Your presence, impressive

Your smile, captivating

Your passion for life, infectious

Your intelligence, superlative

Your character, admirable

The essence of all that is amazing

No one — absolutely *no one* — compares to you

Believe In Your Greatness

Celebrate You!

Embrace all you have come to know, love, and appreciate about your indwelling greatness. Honor your worth, celebrate your presence, live your truth, and let your light shine brightly for all the world to see. *That is your greatness in action!*

I Stand

Statuesque!
Affirming my existence and worthiness

The sparkle in my eyes will continue to shine
when speaking of love and its power
for I personify that of which I speak

The value of my wisdom
transcends time

The abiding faith I once desired
is the faith I now exude

I am a woman of greatness

I know *exactly* who I am
and *where I stand.*

Stay In Touch With Yourself

Set the tone for your day. The attitude of choice is yours. Be a motivator, an encourager, a trailblazer. Aspire to inspire!

Keep it mellow, keep it simple, and with all diligence, do your best to keep negative energy away from your heart.

Be grateful for everyone and everything that enriches your life. Pay it forward!

Give a round of applause for the good fortune of another. It's the perfect *feel good* moment!

Be loving even when it's not reciprocated. Appreciate the ability to be your greater self and stand radiantly in your dwelling place of unconditional love.

Laugh heartily at yourself! It's a miraculous stress reliever and one of the simplest ways to create balance in your life.

Take a staycation. Enjoy your home's surroundings: they are a comforting reflection of you and they inspire appreciation for your many blessings.

Remember the three Rs. *Relax* your mind. *Release* your fears. *Relate* to whatever inspires your soul.

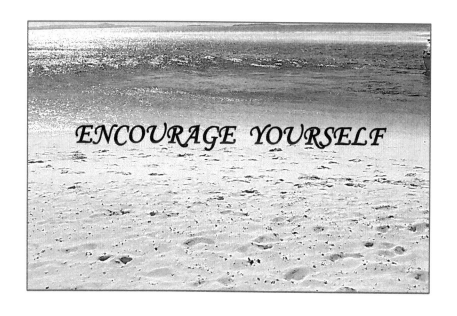

Nurture Your Heart with Sunshine

Swelling tear ducts release liquid sunshine to comfort your heart.

Stress is a normal part of life and everyone experiences it on some level. However, shouldering intense stress is extremely unhealthy and the effects can be harmful to your heart, mind, body, and spirit. Furthermore, buried or concealed anxieties rarely remain incognito — they will inevitably reveal their presence in other damaging ways.

An intuitive aspect of embracing your greatness is knowing what you need and when you need it. Releasing tears is merely another way to self-soothe, to relieve the discomfort of your heart, and to express your deepest feelings. Let your tears flow freely and unashamedly. Let them do what they are designed by God to do: *comfort your heart.*

Seasons change. Although your current season may be stressful, the next could be one of great celebration. Set your heart at ease by embracing this encouraging affirmation: *"This, too, shall pass."*

Liquid Sunshine

God has an endearing way
of providing comfort for your heart

He's blessed you with liquid sunshine
to help wash away your pain

Precious waters of refreshment
flow from your heart
shower over your worries
and clear the path for sunnier days

Your tears are dear to God
not a single teardrop is left unattended
each is tenderly caressed
and held close to His heart

Take a Second Look

When you are in the thick of things, meaningful details that could help
enlighten your perspective are sometimes overlooked.
Step back, regroup, and take another look!

A fair share of time is expended mulling over regrets and past mistakes. Sometimes a second look is all that's needed to be content with your judgment call.

Think about a particular choice you've made that you wished you had the chance to remake. Although it's not physically possible to turn back the hands of time for a *do-over*, it is possible to revise your perspective.

Step back, regroup, and take a second look. Focus on the positive outcomes of your decision. Perchance you'll find the choice you made isn't as disconcerting as you once thought.

Easy Does It

You made a good choice here
an important decision there
and a few mistakes along the way

Sincere intentions of the heart
are sometimes met
with one's own unfair criticism

Thankfully, life graciously presents
far more commas than periods
and far more graces than judgments

When pangs of regret
wrestle with your conscience

Step away
take a nice, deep breath
and revisit your decision

at a later time...

Give Yourself a Pep Talk

The well-guarded conversations of your soul create a sacred reservoir from which to draw inspiring nourishment.

Whether from a beloved family member or a dear friend, now and then we all can use a well-timed Pep Talk. But, have you ever given yourself a Pep Talk — especially when you felt as though you wanted to throw in the towel?

This is where another incredible aspect of your greatness rises to the occasion! Inherently, you are beautifully hardwired to pursue Divine inspiration — encouragement from God when you're at your wits' end. Giving yourself a Pep Talk is an instinctive way to plug into that intimate heavenly realm of inspiration.

So remember, when you're feeling a little less than your best, don't let feelings of discouragement shatter your confidence. *Have the talk!*

Inquiries of the Heart

Dear God,

What inspired you to tailor my being
in the manner that you so lovingly have

What were the reasons you adorned me
with such an incredible mind, endearing heart
and exceptional existence

Why was I given the ability to comprehend
being my own woman

You graced me with great dignity and honor

You endowed me with ever-increasing wisdom
and a measure of faith
that reveals the backbone of my character

You even gave me a sense of humor to amuse me
when I might otherwise feel like crying

And when I feel as though I'm at my wits' end
Your presence rescues my heart and revives my soul

Don't Fret the "Pause"

Opportunities aren't missed,
they're just waiting for the perfect time to make your acquaintance.

There will be times in your life when you'll experience what may best be referred to as *the pause*.

Think of the pause as a duration of silence in which it feels as though everything in your life is being held at bay. In actuality, this interval may have a higher purpose, offering you a necessary span of time to prepare for the next opportunity, experience, or adventure to grace your path.

Moreover, a duration of silence is the perfect interlude to recall answered prayers. The time of reflection will surely produce a defining moment in your faith walk.

Don't fret the pause! Instead, surrender your uncertainties through prayer and patience. Both will help settle your angst and create a refreshing state of peacefulness.

Long Awaited

time has a mysterious way of existing
it can appear to move hastily,
other times it moves at a snail's pace

in the scheme of it all
you've no choice
but to patiently wait for the moment
when all is in perfect alignment
and majestically through the heavens
God shines a beacon of light your way

leaving you to joyfully concede

that it was *all*

well worth

the wait

Have Faith Your Dream Will Come True

Allow your faith to manifest your vision
Sparkle throughout the mist of uncertainty
Glisten throughout the notion of possibility
For happiness is the satisfying fruit of inspiration
Triumph is the harvest of fervor
and fearless determination

Is there a dream near and dear to your heart? Do you find yourself thinking, *if only it were true?* The remarkable reality is that dreams actually *do* come true!

Let me encourage you to:

Endorse your dreams! Aspirations keep you in touch with the essence of who you are. They motivate you to venture out, to experience new and gratifying endeavors.

Nurture your dreams with great faith and great courage; they are remarkable inner strengths that keep your dreams alive and flourishing!

Remain optimistic! Optimism enables you to view temporary setbacks as stepping stones to achieving greater goals.

Your dream may not materialize exactly as you hoped, and that's okay. The awesome blessing is that you were, in fact, *dreaming.*

Transcendent Faith

Delve deeply into the realm of your imagination

Dream marvelous dreams
found in the smallest wisp of inspiration

Explore your unique style
engage your talents and abilities

Observe in awe as your dreams take shape
and elevate to heights
that were hitherto inconceivable

Take a Breather

Focus on yourself for a change.
Surely you're worth more than a momentary glance.

Time to do some unpacking — of your heart! It's been filled to the brim with all sorts of concerns. Your concerns, their concerns, everybody's concerns. *Enough already.* It's totally permissible to take a breather and concentrate specifically on you.

As compassionate women, we have a tendency to take on the cares of the world. We make it our faithful mission to help it, fix it, cure it, or save it. However, in the midst of our genuine efforts to be everything to everyone, our hearts are inundated with a checklist of worries. How then are we to find *breathing room* for ourselves? Here's how:

Plan timeouts for self-care and rejuvenation.

Nourish your heart with an extra measure of gratitude for life.

Inspire yourself through an avenue of prayer and meditation.

Enliven your mind with inspirational readings and positive affirmations.

Increase your energy level with an energizing activity such as walking, yoga, or swimming.

Awaken your senses with an invigorating shower or bath using your favorite fragrances.

Rechannel your energies.

Frequent a quiet bookstore. Saunter down the aisles of your choice, curl up in a comfy chair, and enjoy some of your favorite books.

Try on that stunning outfit you've been eyeing for months. Any day is a perfect retail therapy day!

Treat yourself to lunch. Try something on the menu you wouldn't ordinarily indulge in. Do the same for dinner, and don't leave out dessert! This is *not* the day to pour on the guilt.

Relax, Release, and Relate.

Be content in the company of one. Spend time alone and love it.

Take a breather! Don't allow your heart to be consumed with anxious care. Give yourself permission to be free of emotional entanglement. Know that your earnest prayers on behalf of those near and dear to your heart is caring, and, is enough.

Connect with the people, places, and things that inspire and encourage you to unwind, re-center, and be fully present in all your greatness.

Timeout!

Wait a minute, stop, slow down
You are moving much too fast

Your body is on fast forward
your thoughts are on rewind
and your heart is set to record

You can't seem to locate the exhale
that's supposed to follow your inhale

The roller coaster of life
never seems to coast
only to accelerate
and your nerves are wearing thin

Take a breather!

Bring *everything* to a standstill
focus on you *alone*

Relax In Abundant Peace

Inhale. Exhale. Pause. Repeat.

Create a harmonious space in your home where you and peace are the sole occupants. Your space can be an entire room, a section of a room, a spacious closet, or wherever you choose. Rest there, totally free of time constraints. Make sure your space is void of unnecessary stuff and filled with meaningful belongings, smells, colors, sights, and sounds that echo the affections of your heart and attest to the remarkable woman you are.

You'll want to linger in this intimate space of peace for a while. Tarry — stay as long as you need to because you *will* need to! We all need time and space just *to be.*

In your space of peace, you can choose to engage in private devotion, listen to soft music, read an inspiring book, journal, take a soothing, effervescent bath, or simply lose yourself in the blessedness of peace. Be still: don't crowd your space or allow anyone else to. Do yourself a well-deserved favor and rest comfortably in your solitude, as it is exactly the destination that's been awaiting your arrival. Be altogether present and relax in your abundant peace.

Quiet, Please

Enter into your secluded retreat

Delay all interruptions
set them aside
for however long

Right now
it's all about you

You can
if you choose

You may
or you may not

Do whatever you like
or nothing at all

Preserve Your Calmness

Silence is golden — and necessary.

With so much disorder in our world today, it's sometimes difficult to maintain serenity. What people desire most is the ability to remain centered and calm in the midst of chaos. On your journey to embracing your greatness, preserving your calmness is essential.

Here are some helpful recommendations:

Reserve and honor your downtime. It's your time to do with as you please. Fill it with more pleasure and less stress; more silence and less unnecessary noise.

Try to avoid handling major concerns unless you've had a proper night's rest. It's vitally important to relax your body as well as your mind. Making decisions when you are sleep-deprived may not produce the best outcome.

Although there is amazement in the way you are able to juggle so many things simultaneously, you are certainly not *Super Woman*. Recognize that now and again you need to let it go — whatever *it* happens to be.

Incorporate activities into your life that promote peace, joy, relaxation, and wellbeing, such as mini-vacations, special outings, a walk along the seashore, a soothing massage, and the all-important *me time*. These are must-have restorative engagements.

Cool, Calm, and Collected

In my state of calmness
comforting peace
permeates every fiber of my existence

I'm present and composed

My mind and heart are occupied
with tranquility

There's no vacancy for discontentment

At this very moment
all that I am and have
is everything I need

My heart is at peace
my mind is at ease

All is well with my soul

Nourish Your Soul

When God awakens you in dawning hours for a heavenly feast
of His creation, rest assured He has prepared sufficient wonderment
to nourish your soul for more than a single setting.

As the sun makes its glorious appearance just over the horizon, a plethora of amazement unfolds. Birds fly joyfully about the heavens, the wind blows softly and peacefully where it pleases, the flowers gently unfold to greet the misty dew and a fresh fragrance lingers in the air.

Alluring presentations of wonder exquisitely bestowed for your nourishment. *Bon appetit!*

Nature's Concerto

The splendor of an early morning symphony
needs no arranging or fine tuning

Each instrument of praise compliments the heavens

The participants are honored to present
their song of adoration
to an attentive audience

A harmonious and inviting composition
a serenade of joyful adulation from
Creation to Creator

Beautify a Life

A breath of fresh air is Heaven's inspiration
and humanity's consolation.

A woman's voice is remarkably gifted: expressive, soothing nurturing, intriguing, and graceful are just a few of the many adjectives that describe her voice and its natural ability to brighten an individual's day. Frequently used expressions such as *Hello, Good morning, Thank you, How are you?* and especially, *I love you*, caress the heart when graciously communicated.

Someone needs to feel a breath of fresh air today. Your voice could be the breeze that comforts and inspires simply because it's pleasant, filled with warmth, and conveyed with a smile.

A Gracious Utterance

To a lonely heart
it speaks of belonging

To an empty countenance
it speaks of worthiness

To an angry outburst
it speaks of temperance

To a loving heart
it speaks the same language

Blessings of inspiration
flow from your expressions

Beautify a life!

Plant Seeds of Kindness

Build hope.
Encourage love.
Be understanding.
These are the kindnesses our hearts thirst for.

If there is one prized possession the world needs more of, it's kindness. Having said that, it's rather effortless to extend kindness when others are kind to you. But what could possibly inspire you to demonstrate kindness to someone who's unkind?

Three very good reasons instantly come to mind:

The *first reason* is because it's a declaration of your inherent goodness. A goodness that actually longs to be expressed! Each expression of kindness creates great satisfaction for the soul long after the act.

The *second reason* is because of the kindnesses you have received. If you took a comprehensive survey of your life and attempted to tally up the various benevolences you've been granted, there's *no way* you could remember them all!

The *third reason* is because sincere kindness remains an effective approach to reconciling differences. It's a bridge of hope, love, and understanding. Make it your ambition to cross over this superbly crafted walkway every opportunity you have.

The Real Deal

No artificial or added ingredients
All natural, pure, and authentic

Its source is from ancient beginnings
A heavenly food, a delightful delicacy

It lightens many burdens
Heals many wounds of the soul
Makes merry the most hardened of hearts
Bridges differences and dissolves discord

Kindness
One of life's most enjoyable and rewarding pleasures

Leave a Lasting Impression

Speak words of genuine encouragement.
The footprints you leave on the heart of the listener will last forever.

Words leave lasting impressions. Some impressions are inspiring while others are quite the contrary. A woman of greatness is keenly aware of the influence her words have. Thus, her *sweet inspirations* are well-chosen. She exercises discretion and infuses her words with genuine compassion and encouragement so the heart readily absorbs their nurturing intent. Her motive is always to inspire.

As well, she knows how to respond with diplomacy when confronted with an unkind remark. Her temperate response will speak volumes as to the virtue of her character. After all, she's a representation of graciousness!

You've undoubtedly heard the statement, "It's not what you say, it's how you say it." Actually, careful consideration should be given to what is said as well as how it is said. The listener is inspired (or unfortunately, uninspired) by the nature of the conversation as well as the tone of delivery.

Make the impression you leave on the listener's heart your greatest concern.

Captive Audience

Desperately hanging on to every word

Listening intently for the utterance
that will bring peace, hope, and joy
to my torn, worn, and weary soul

Listening for exhilaration
inspiration
adoration

Listening for something
anything
that tells me I matter to you

Savor the Moment

Appreciate your blessings.
Gratitude will pave the way for future seasons of refreshment.

Life is filled with exceptional moments, unforgettable points in time that remain close to the heart. In savoring the moment, you are blessed to relive timeless and meaningful memories time and again. Be grateful for the gift of remembrance and let each delightful sentiment water the garden of your heart.

With that being said, your family and friends are very precious gifts; make sure you are attentive to their interests. Embrace those opportune times to create *oodles* of fond memories for all to enjoy for years to come!

Sentimental Journey

Winsome smiles
familiar voices, hearty laughter
endearing embraces

Flashbacks of celebratory events
impressive accomplishments
fulfilled dreams

Treasured moments of life —
such joy they bring

FOR THE GREATER GOOD

Appreciate Your Cheering Squad

If you sit quietly on the sidelines,
you just might miss your chance to make a resounding difference.

You have an amazing cheering squad! These are the people who encourage you to keep the faith, to never give up, and to expect a brighter tomorrow. Their hearts are excited about the blessings destined to greet your life. They are the ones who lift your spirit and leave you smiling long after they've left your presence.

Moreover, they look forward to hearing your voice on the other end of the phone and are delighted to fill your cup with encouragement. They are quite happy to be your cheering squad simply because you've poured bountifully into their lives as well.

On those occasions when you feel as though you haven't got a cheering squad, don't be discouraged. As long as you continue to be an inspiration to others, your personal *ensemble of encouragers* are sure to arrive at your door, and all in perfect time.

Magnificent Ensemble

Stars inspire dreams beyond the visual

Mountain-tops give vivid hope
to the attainment of the unfathomable

The vastness of the ocean
encourages endless enthusiasm

The brilliance of the sun and the shine of the moon
shed beautiful light into the vestibules of the heart

Your presence echoes their wonderment!

Ambitions don't seem as far-fetched
when viewed through the lens
of your encouragement

When I'm betwixt and between a mountain of fears
your loving advice inspires me
to look beyond my doubts, to reach for the stars

Like subtle ocean waves
I hear your comforting voice
when my voice is non-existent

When dark clouds hover over my world
the brightness of your optimism
shines through

Celebrate Togetherness

One of the most inspiring places to be is in the presence
of an extraordinary woman.
Her heart represents a true spirit of love.

There's a definite heart-to-heart connection among women. Although we live in distant lands, have different skin colors, represent different cultures, honor different beliefs, and speak different languages, we are *agents of harmony,* which enables us to respect and embrace our diversities from a perspective of oneness.

Women are a powerful assortment of incredible essence and one of the greatest blessings on Earth!

Resembling Hearts

We share a kindred spirit, unique
and yet alike on many levels

We stand collectively in separate spaces of existence
and yet we stand on equal turf

We share similar hopes and dreams
for ourselves, our family, and our friends

We uphold each other!

Together we are a threefold cord
a strength to be revered
a seamless blend of heart, mind, and soul

Aspire to Inspire

All eyes are on you!
Carpe Diem!

Enthusiastic hearts are presented with immeasurable occasions to inspire. When your excitement is high-spirited, it spills over into someone else's path of hope. Look for those ever-present windows of opportunity to be someone's shining star; they are indeed looking to the high heavens for you!

Shining Example

Through the windows of your eyes
I see optimism, courage, and resolve

You motivate me to believe
I have the wings to fly
I have what it takes to succeed

Thank you for your gift of
enthusiasm, tenacity, and spirit

Thank you for the open invitation
to glean from your lovely garden
of inspiration

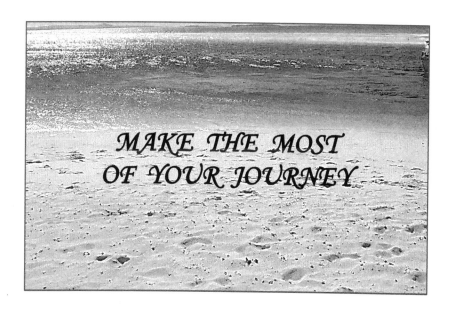

MAKE THE MOST
OF YOUR JOURNEY

Move Forth Fearlessly

Your trepidation has been working overtime.
It's high time you retire it!

Fear and feeling inadequate prevent many women from embarking on remarkable paths created specifically for them. Both these emotions burden the heart, create undeserved pressure, and impede progress. Surprisingly, however, the same emotions can actually motivate you to *rise above* such unnerving obstacles!

Truth be told, when it comes to moving forth fearlessly, many of us could benefit from an extra portion of faith in our abilities. One way to conquer your fears is to take a chance. Leap enthusiastically into the desires of your heart and observe how your landing is divinely supported by all God has planned for you.

When you are on the path designed specifically for you, marvelous revelations unfold to prepare and empower you to *move forth fearlessly*.

Awesome peace overtakes you.

Fears fade.

Feelings of inadequacy depart.

Courage is employed.

Self-confidence increases.

Your inner voice is the inspiration of your heart and the influence of your soul. Listen closely; do not allow apprehension to muffle their presence. Trust in your God-given abilities, move forth in faith, and welcome your breakthrough!

Courageous Heart

It's a long journey into the depths of my soul
and I've been walking endlessly

I've walked paths of self-doubt
and roamed hallways of timidity

I've traversed terrains of inner turbulence
and tested my physical limitations

Nevertheless

I'd walk an eternity
if it meant the journey's end
was the gathering place of my faith

There,
fear is nonexistent!

Make It a Great Day

It's a brand new day and you've been given a blank canvas.
Now what?

We'd all like to have a great day. But to make your day great, you need to give it your personal touch. That means designing and arranging your day to be as spectacular as you choose.

Just for a second, think about the things you believe need to happen for your day to be great. Is your participation required or are you depending on others to provide the essentials? The fact of the matter is, you hold the key to your heart, and therefore you know what inspires it. Invite those inspirations to fashion a *sensational day!*

There's a flip side, however. The day could begin on a positive note and yet, much to your dismay, something unforeseen infringes upon your peace and joy. Granted, it may very well be something that would cause anyone's day to be altered from great to unpleasant. Remember, you maintain the choice as to how you allow that particular occurrence to influence your demeanor, your actions, your outlook, and your day.

As you are designing your day, remember to:

Keep it simple. Don't begin the day bombarding your mind with a congested "To Do" list.

Expect the unexpected to interrupt your day every now and then. When it does, breathe, remain centered, and calmly handle what you can, as best you can.

Revisit the key points listed on page 18, "Stay In Touch With Yourself." They'll provide ample food for thought to help you create a truly great day.

Masterful Fashionista

Decorate the day to *your* liking
Embellish it with all *your* favorites
Whatever makes *your* heart joyful, embrace it

Create an environment that showcases
your taste, *your* vision,
your distinct personality

One that suits *you* perfectly

Give this day *your* very own consent
to be great!

Invest In Yourself

Make it your priority to be your priority!

Have you ever promised yourself something and somehow life got in the way and your desire to fulfill that promise evaporated? Take heart, because you are certainly not alone. Many have walked a similar path. And although your enthusiasm has taken a back seat, I'd venture to say the passion yet remains. Let it inspire and empower you to honor your oath as the priority it once was.

Belief, faith, and perseverance are the cornerstones of inner wealth. Do your best to prioritize your life and leave no stone unturned in fulfilling your commitment to yourself.

You're not so far out of touch with your plans; you just took a brief hiatus!

Priority Status!

We alter our schedule
Put our plans on hold
Elect to get in where we fit in

In the midst of it all
we somehow manage
to get lost in the shuffle

What's a woman to do?

Elevate yourself to the *top* of the list
Pray for persevering faith
Immerse yourself in your passion
Work through temporary distractions

Most important
carve out recharging interludes

Before long —
You've successfully *reclaimed*
your priority status!

Get Up and Go!

Self-reinvention is an amplified version of yourself.

It all begins with you. If you have an earnest desire to reinvent yourself, you will. Perhaps you want to give new energies to an interest that's been buried in the toils of vacillation much too long. It's time to remove the cobwebs and go for it. Be optimistic. Awaken and embrace your natural creative abilities, stay prayerful, and "Get Up and Go!"

Be mindful, however, that when you are on the road to self-reinvention, doubt has a way of creeping in to undermine your good efforts. An effective way to circumvent *bouts of doubt* is to get ahead of the game. Begin your reinvention journey with the end destination in sight. Your vision and "Get Up and Go!" attitude will fuel your determination to succeed. Doors of opportunity will begin to open widely even if you haven't yet begun to knock!

It's important you remember that reinventing yourself doesn't happen overnight. It takes time, conviction, preparation, fearlessness, nurturance, and staying power. When the time is right, you'll definitely make a salient reemergence — all because you possessed the heart, ingenuity, and drive to "Get Up and Go!"

Amplified Version

Nestled deep within your womanly frame
is an exuberant spirit, a visionary

The fullness of your passion
is an ever-burning flame
igniting a drive that yearns fulfillment

Whether completely alone
or in a dense crowd
you project confidence, courage, pizzazz

Motivated, focused, and poised
you ascend to magnificent zeniths
of personal evolution

You are living your purpose

and living it

stupendously!

Embrace Your New Horizon

New horizons are unexpected doors of opportunity!
They affirm the reality of unimaginable godsends.

You are in store for a life-changing adventure when a new horizon enters your world. Unbeknownst to you, this potential was evolving in the background of your life long before it ever emerged to grace your path. Amazingly, it unites with the secret desires of your soul, inspires you to spread your wings of enthusiasm, and compels you to soar eagerly toward a magnificent unfolding.

A Distant Spurring

Ever experience a strong sense of knowing
but couldn't quite grasp what inspired
such an intuitive state of awareness?

A powerful spurring!
With yet a quiet gentleness to its presence

The embraceable part of
this soul-stirring phenomenon
is your miraculous ability to sense your inside voice
heralding the advent of your new horizon

A delectable foretaste of destiny!

Enjoy the Sweet Milestones along the Way

Revel in your blessings.
Indulge in how they sweeten your life!

Milestones are noteworthy personal achievements; they say something fascinating and historic about your life's journey!

Take care not to resign your milestones to the last rung on your ladder of gratitude. Celebrate their significance in grand fashion the rest of your life!

Your Attention, Please!

Moments are fleeting,
here today, gone today

Take not for granted
the gift of the rising sun
or the going down of the same

Pay close attention to
what makes you smile, laugh, or even sigh,
to what makes you pause, gasp, or cry

Cherish the blessings that make you wish
there were more than twenty-four hours in a day

For they are the *sweet milestones*
lovingly placed for you to enjoy
along your way

Sweet Milestones...

Add More Humor to Your Life

Good old-fashioned bellyaching laughter is hearty food for the soul!

Life has its share of challenges. Some are gratifying and others chip away at the very joys of your soul. It is important, however, that you learn to enjoy the lighter side of life and to take things a little less seriously. Believe it or not, challenges and humor do occasionally coexist! But to appreciate the latter, you need only to make room.

Check out these light-hearted ideas!

Try singing to yourself! Whether you can or can't carry a tune doesn't really matter. It's purely for your own entertainment and enjoyment. Sing in the shower, in your car, and in your home when everyone is gone. Turn up the volume on your radio and sing along with your favorite musician. Loudly! Do this especially when you don't know all the words to the song; it's hilarity at its highest level!

Dance! Dance to your own rhythm. Who cares who's watching? Perhaps in watching you, they'll let loose and experience their own happy!

Spend a day watching your favorite movies. The ones you watch over and over and laugh as though you've never seen the movie before!

Or perhaps there's something you once enjoyed doing that you no longer do. Give new life to those tucked-away pastimes, especially if they are amusing.

Just One

Side-clenching
Eye-watering
Air-gasping
Knee-slapping
Uncontrollable laugh

Is enough to make you forget
all about your *whatevers*

So laugh!

Until your blahs wane
Your cheeks ache
And your cares slowly fade

away...

Just Be You

The magnifying glass is a very useful device,
but it was not created for you to be placed under!

Who, pray tell, ever said you had to be perfect? In fact, what exactly does it mean to be perfect? Who has the monopoly on defining perfection? Many have come under scrutiny for not fitting the mold, not measuring up, or not satisfying someone else's lofty expectations.

Just be you. That's all! And should you happen upon someone trying to revamp your uniqueness, feel free to disregard their audacity in your own gracious way. What's more, just in case you need a refresher as to *everything* there is to love about you, I believe you'll find the following poem a luscious rendering.

You Are

The Crème de la Crème
Best of the best
Second to none
Incapable of being duplicated

You Are

In tune with your life, voice, and measure of greatness
A woman of incredible intelligence and splendor
An ever-evolving inspiration of your choosing

You Are

Absolutely more estimable than others or society
guesstimate you to be

You Are

All that
and then some!

BE AN ENDURING LIGHT

Create a Legacy of Love

Love is truly the gift that keeps on giving.
Everything is always about love.

A woman has an innate ability that enables her to extend compassion to people from all walks of life. Going the extra mile to make a lasting difference in someone's world is not difficult for her. Her life's work is to leave a loving imprint on the hearts of those whom she's had the pleasure of knowing. For these reasons and so many more, she aptly dons the esteemed badge of honor termed *greatness*!

Create your legacy of love! Engrave the pages of your life with genuine love, tenderness, joy, peace, encouragement, and wisdom so that generation to generation is blessed to experience the warmth of your enduring light.

Rainbow Love

A woman's love is like
the magnificent colors of a rainbow

Vivid, breathtaking, inspiring,
miraculous, and refreshing
a solid flow of matchless splendor

Not even a gloomy day
can prevent the intensity of her love
from shining through

That's
the glorious legacy of a woman's love

Share Your Story

Personal transparency is not an undertaking for the faint of heart.
It challenges one to be selfless, fearless, and crystal clear.

We all have a story to tell. Are you willing to share yours, no holds barred? Those who know you well have a front row seat into the essence of who you are. But what about the women who aren't in your immediate circle of family and friends? They're the dear hearts clamoring to hear that there's someone in this world who can actually relate to their feelings about love, life, disappointments, hopes, and dreams.

They want to look deep into the eyes of the woman who's been there and done that. The woman who's willing to be open and honest about her personal tests and trials as well as her great strides. They're searching for the woman who will be their advocate, their voice, their mirror.

They're searching for you!

They want to know you genuinely care about their plight in life.

They want to feel the comfort of placing their head on the strength of your shoulders.

When an extra measure of reassurance and love is needed, it's your tender embrace they want to feel.

It's your adoring face they yearn to envision when the faces before them have the appearance of neither gentleness nor concern.

You certainly have a story to tell. And it is one that cannot fully be told without paying homage to the women who have poured invaluable lessons into your life. They have passed the baton and along with it the grand opportunity to mirror their tribute and amazing sacrifices. These extraordinary women deserve great recognition: let your life be an echoing testament to their worth. Share your story unafraid. Someone needs to be refreshed by it.

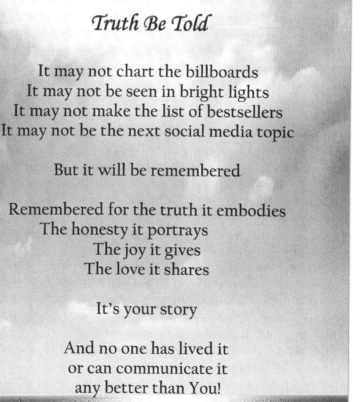

Truth Be Told

It may not chart the billboards
It may not be seen in bright lights
It may not make the list of bestsellers
It may not be the next social media topic

But it will be remembered

Remembered for the truth it embodies
The honesty it portrays
The joy it gives
The love it shares

It's your story

And no one has lived it
or can communicate it
any better than You!

Journal Your Journey

This is your phenomenal journey:
why not get up close and personal with it?

Seldom do we have time throughout the course of a day to pause and reflect on the various details contained therein. So much of life is crammed into our schedule that sometimes the more meaningful components are placed on hold or buried amongst a gamut of activities — never having received our full attention.

Which is why spending quiet time in the pages of your journal should be a welcome end to your day. It's when you get to pause, unwind, and get up close and personal with your life. Retire to the harmonious space of peace you created for yourself; it's the ideal setting to ruminate.

If you choose not to journal every day, consider the end of the week as an option. Be as detailed as you can. Make sure to capture those extraordinary occurrences you don't want left to memory alone. Your veracity should leap off the pages!

Writing down your thoughts is an authentic form of self-expression and a relaxing way to settle into your evening.

Heart Contemplations

It's the end of a very long day
and you're feeling spent,
You desire nothing more than to pamper yourself
with some much deserved rest and relaxation

You take a soothing bubble bath
enjoy a deliciously appealing meal
and sip a nice warm cup of your favorite tea

You fluff the pillows on your freshly scented bed
snuggle in comfortably
and play a soft melody to lull yourself to sleep

But, before drifting off to bask
in your luxurious private oasis
there's just one other must-do

Your heart could use some attending to!

Surely the events of the day have served up
a few tasty morsels of inspiration worthy of treasuring
what better place to preserve their worth
than on the pages of that lovely journal
resting on your nightstand

In later years when your mind takes
a stroll down memory lane
yearning to recall a particular breath of time,
your timeless reflections will be noted sweetly
within the pressed leaves of an irreplaceable jewel

Your friend, your confidante, your journal.

Be Grateful

Embrace your past
filled with its gathering of peaks and valleys
for they are the whys and wherefores
that color the canvas of your life so majestically

Be grateful for fortitude
to rise above disappointment

Grateful for peace
that reigns supreme over adversity

Grateful for confidence
to believe in a brighter day

Grateful for a measure of faith
that extends far beyond reason

Grateful for a Heavenly Power
greater than your own

An Extra Dose of Inspiration

Remember to take a hiatus
from the demands of life
to refresh and replenish your soul.

Love is a continuous embrace of the heart.
When all is said and done,
the power of love *always* prevails.

Approach your dreams with
optimism and gratitude —
they are the roads most traveled
to glorious achievements.

When life fills your cup with more concerns
than you care to swallow,
take smaller sips.

Live, love, and laugh today.
When tomorrow comes,
thankfully duplicate your expressions of praise.

Embrace your indwelling greatness.
Honor your worth.
Always celebrate you!

Engage In Thought

(Relax in your harmonious space of peace)

Which topics encouraged your heart most?

_____

_____

_____

_____

What did you learn about yourself you hadn't appreciated before?

_____

_____

_____

_____

List five inspirations you are enthusiastic to embrace.

_____

_____

_____

_____

_____

Describe your understanding of your greatness after reading *Inspiration for the Heart of a Woman.*

_____
_____
_____
_____

How will you pay forward the encouragement you have received?

_____
_____
_____
_____

Any concluding thoughts?

_____
_____
_____
_____

Let's
Stay Connected!

Website
crystallawrenceinspires.com

Email
crystallawrence.inspires@gmail.com

For Book Orders
(and to post your review!)
Amazon.com

For Your Journaling Pleasure

24349603R10057

Made in the USA
Columbia, SC
21 August 2018